world
AF616620

South America

Find the stickers of the missing animals,
and fill in the names of the places.

a____ falls
parrot
anaconda
toucan
m____ picchu
c_____ the
redeemer
llama
the a____

Africa

camel

giraffe

e______

Middle east
lion
p______
african
elephant
m____
kilimanjaro
zebra
v________
falls
table m________
lemur

Australasia

kangaroo

didgeridoo

koala
bear

great
white shark

clownfish
crocodile
g____
barrier reef
u____
s______
opera house
sheep

North America

moose
niagara f____
buffalo
horse
statue of
l______
rattlesnake

Europe

polar bear
trans-siberian r______
wolf
the a___
the k______
o____ trees
the c_________

Asia

snowy owl
arctic fox
great w___ of china
m____ fuji
forbidden c___
panda
tropical fish

Antarctica

albatross
penguin
south
p___
blue whale

Look back through the book to see where these words appear.

On the
Farm

Big red barn
Can you find and circle five differences between the two pictures?

Woof the Sheepdog!

Woof has lost his herd, can you find the trail that leads to the sheep?

Penny the pony

What colour should Penny be?

Now colour her in.

All things red

Use your pencils or crayons
to colour everything in.

Tractor
Strawberry

Muddy piglets

Which piglet isn't covering himself in mud?

Bernie the bull

Bernie has lost his horns and nose ring!
Can you find the stickers for him?

Duckling bathtime

Can you find the duckling stickers so that mummy duck can see them?

Lost Spots

Molly the cow has lost her spots.
Can you help her by colouring them in?

Partridge in a pear tree

Can you spot the partridge nesting in the orchard?

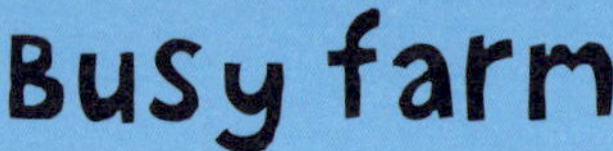

Busy farm

Colour in the tractor and find the sheep stickers to help the farmer round them up.

Harvest time!

Join the dots and colour in the lovely ripe fruit.

Shapes

Square

Find the stickers, trace and colour in the missing shapes.

Chess board
Cushion
Blanket
What colour is the present?
Present
Basket

Circle

Find the stickers, trace and colour in the missing shapes.

Clock

Cookie

Tomato

Ball

How many peas can you count?
Peas
Coin
10
Apple
Button
Wheel

Triangle

Find the stickers, trace and colour in the missing shapes.

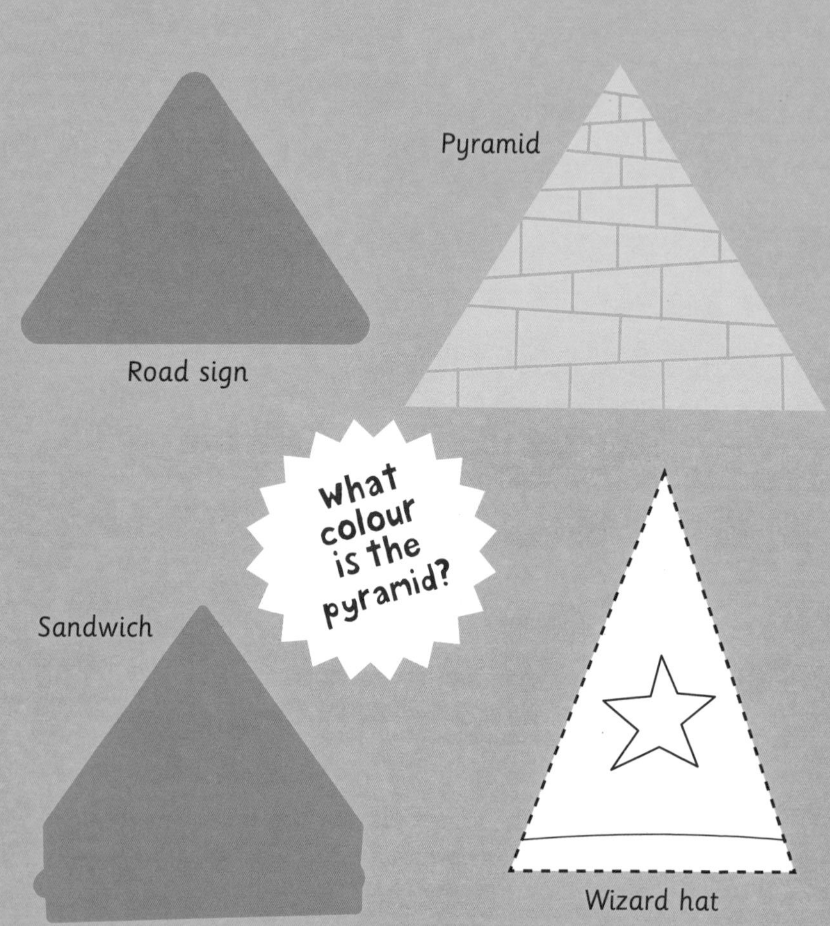

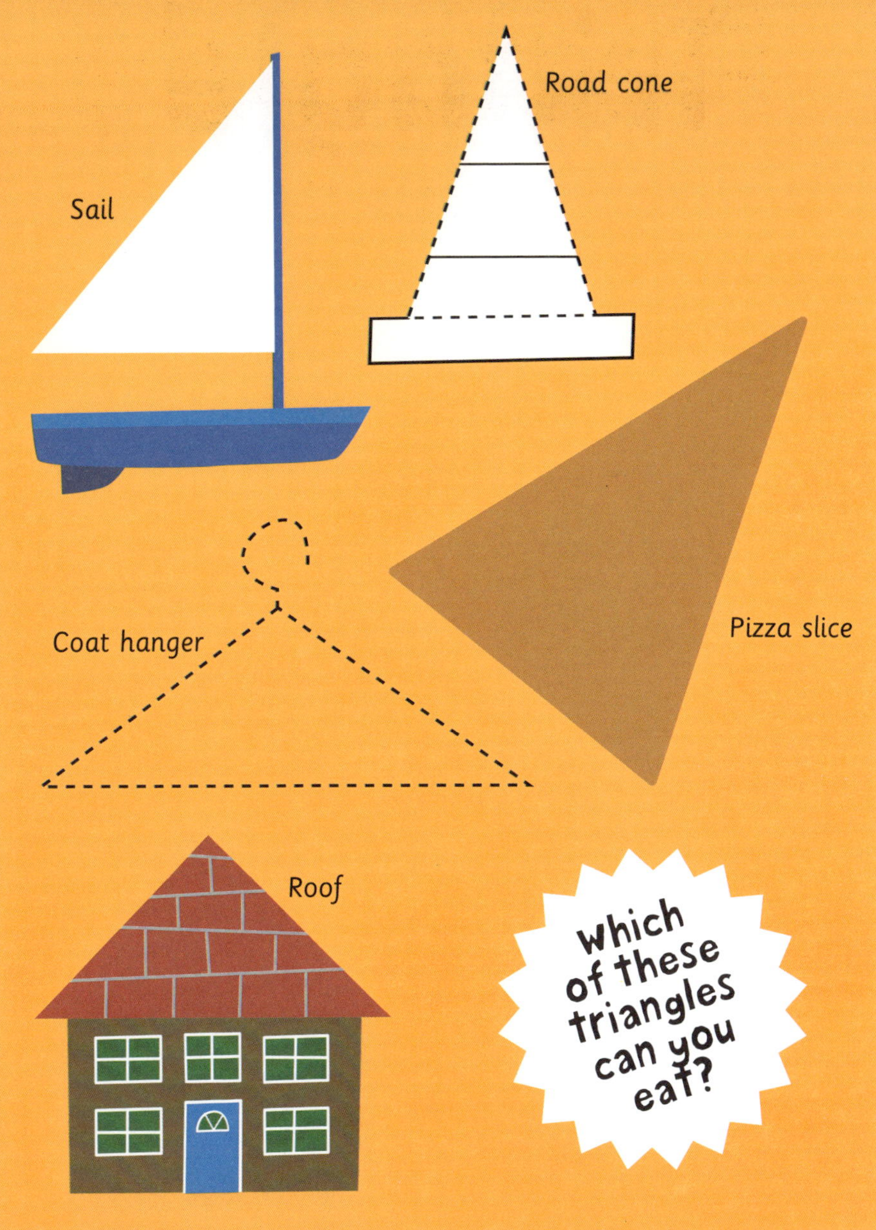
Road cone
Sail
Pizza slice
Coat hanger
Roof
Which of these triangles can you eat?

Rectangle

Find the stickers, trace and colour in the missing shapes.

Picture frame

Briefcase

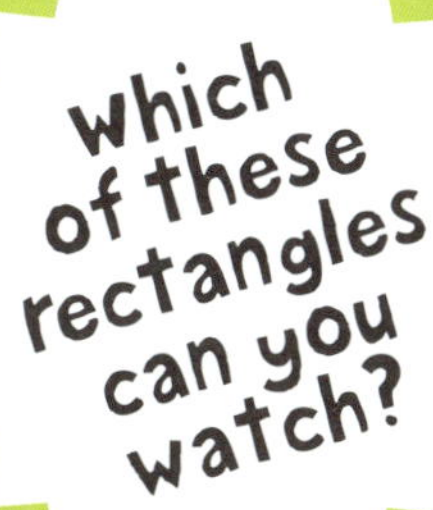

Bank note

Flag

Television

Oval

Find the stickers, trace and colour in the missing shapes.

Star

Find the stickers, trace and colour in the missing shapes.

Space Shapes

Find the shapes in this scene and colour them in.

Home

Find the shapes in this scene and colour them in.

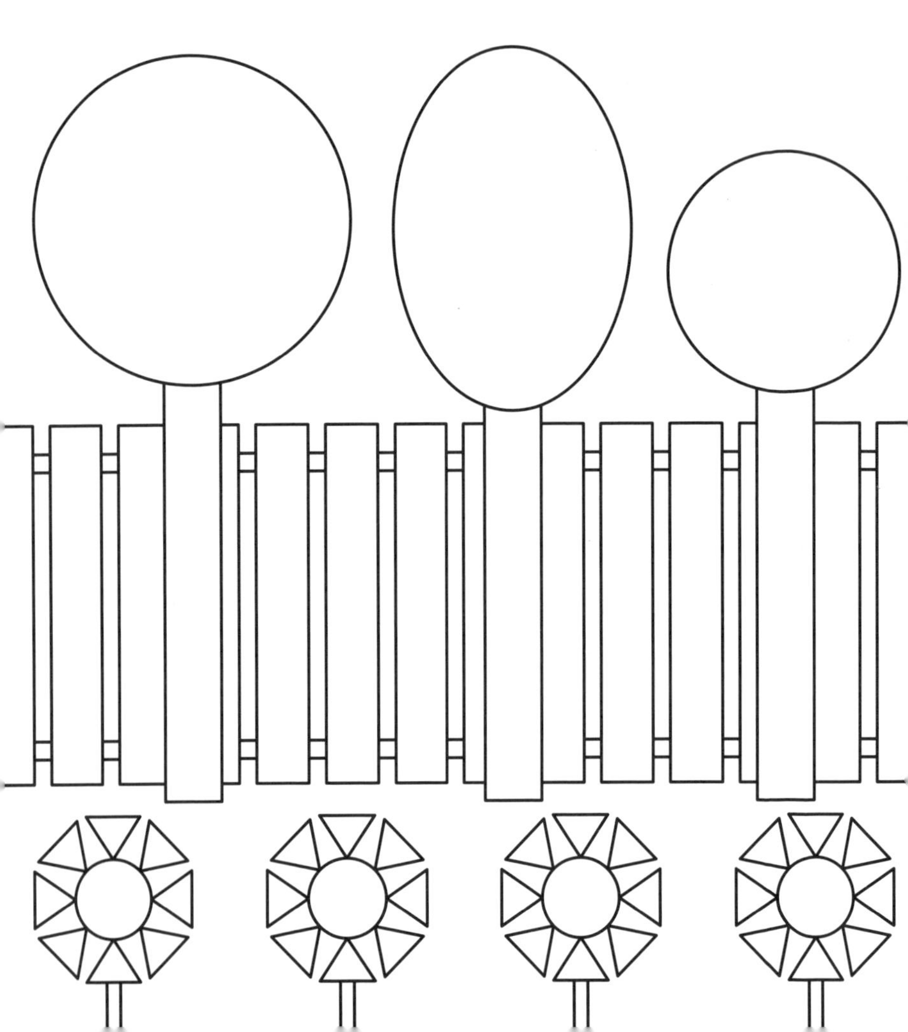

Train

Find the shapes in this scene and colour them in.

The Gingerbread Man

The Gingerbread Man

Once upon a time, an old baker and his wife lived in a cottage near a river. One day the baker decided to bake a gingerbread man. He rolled out the dough, cut out the body and decorated him with raisins and icing for eyes and buttons.

When the baker thought the Gingerbread Man was ready he opened the oven door – and out jumped the Gingerbread Man. He had come to life! "Stop, stop!" shouted the baker and his wife as they chased after the Gingerbread Man, but he was far too fast.

"Run, run, as fast as you can, you can't catch me! I'm the Gingerbread Man!" he shouted back.

Outside the baker's shop, a boy saw the Gingerbread Man. "I'll catch him," he said, and joined the chase.

"Stop, stop!" shouted the baker, his wife and the boy as they chased after the Gingerbread Man, but he was far too fast.

"Run, run, as fast as you can, you can't catch me! I'm the Gingerbread Man!" he shouted back.

In the field, a horse and cow saw the Gingerbread Man. "We'll catch him," they said, and joined the chase. "Stop, stop!" shouted the baker, his wife, the boy, the horse and the cow as they chased after the Gingerbread Man, but he was far too fast.

"Run, run, as fast as you can, you can't catch me! I'm the Gingerbread Man!" he shouted back.

By the river was a sly old fox, who offered to help the Gingerbread Man cross the river. "Jump on my back and I will take you across." So the Gingerbread Man jumped on the fox's back. But as he took him across the river he flicked the Gingerbread Man into the air… and the sly old fox opened his mouth and gobbled him all up!

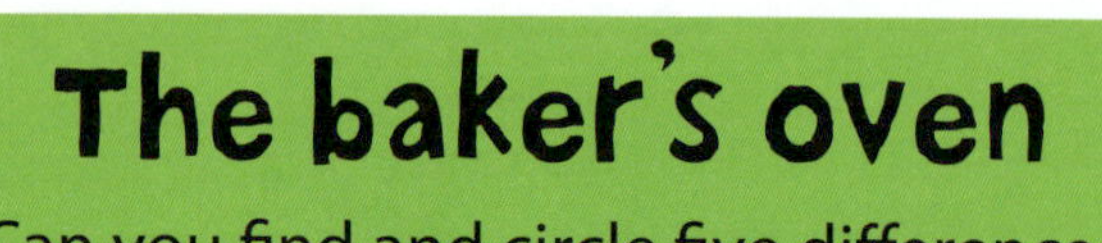

The baker's oven

Can you find and circle five differences between the two pictures?

Match the batch

Find the missing stickers
then trace the lines to join them.

Baker's hat

Join the dots then find stickers to decorate.

The great escape

Find some stickers to complete the scene.

Gingerbread decorations

Find the stickers to complete the Gingerbread Man.

clever old fox

Fox is hungry and would like a gingerbread man!
Can you help him?

Finger puppets

Ask a grown-up to cut us out.

stick us to card
to make us strong!

finish the other activities first!

Matching pairs

Draw lines to join the matching pairs together.

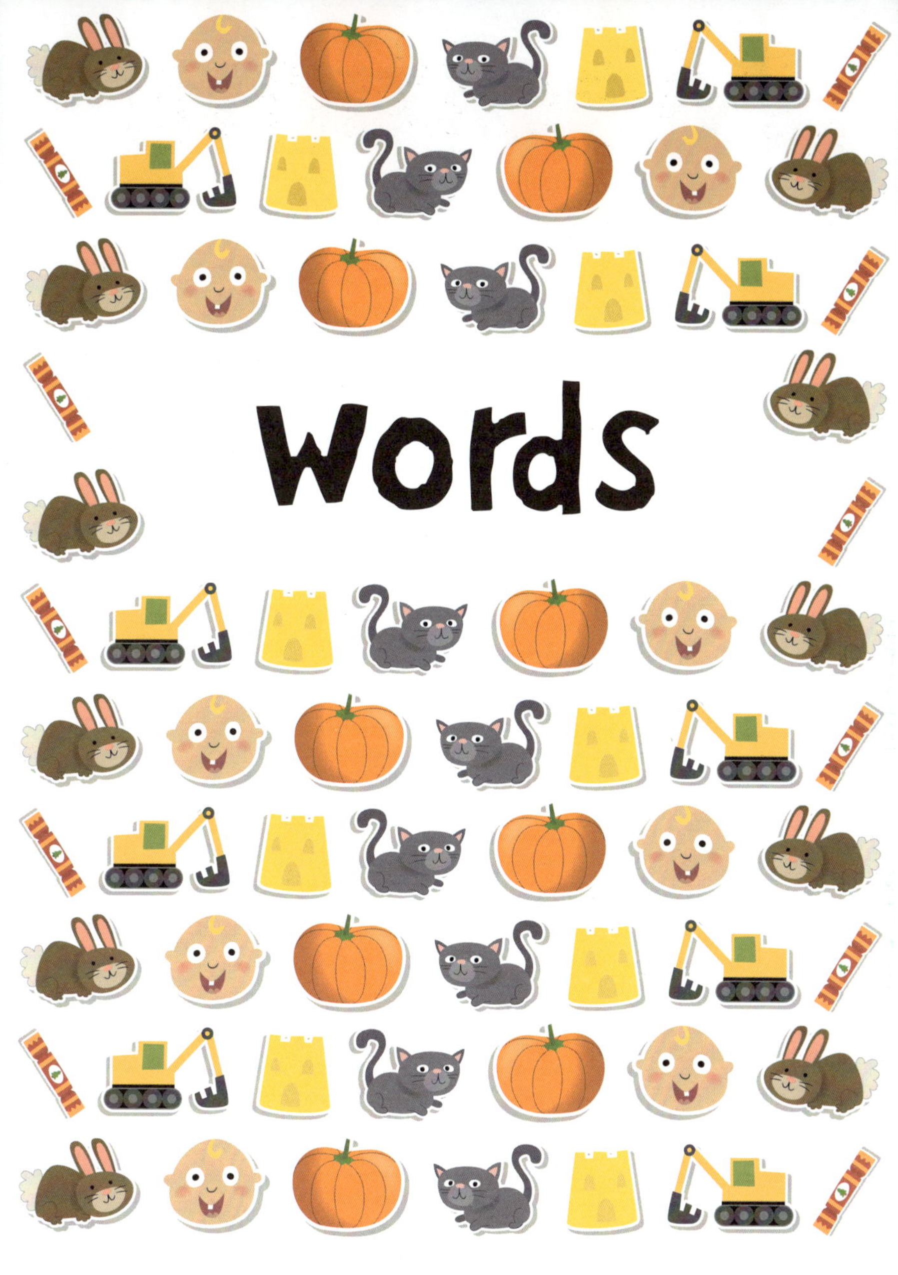

Words

Mealtime

Find the stickers, trace and colour in.

Playtime

Find the stickers, trace and colour in.

Bathtime

Find the stickers, trace and colour in.

Bedtime

Find the stickers, trace and colour in.

Spring

Find the stickers, trace and colour in.

Summer

Find the stickers, trace and colour in.

Autumn

Find the stickers, trace and colour in.

Winter

Find the stickers, trace and colour in.

Garden

Find the stickers, trace and colour in.

Things that go

Find the stickers, trace and colour in.

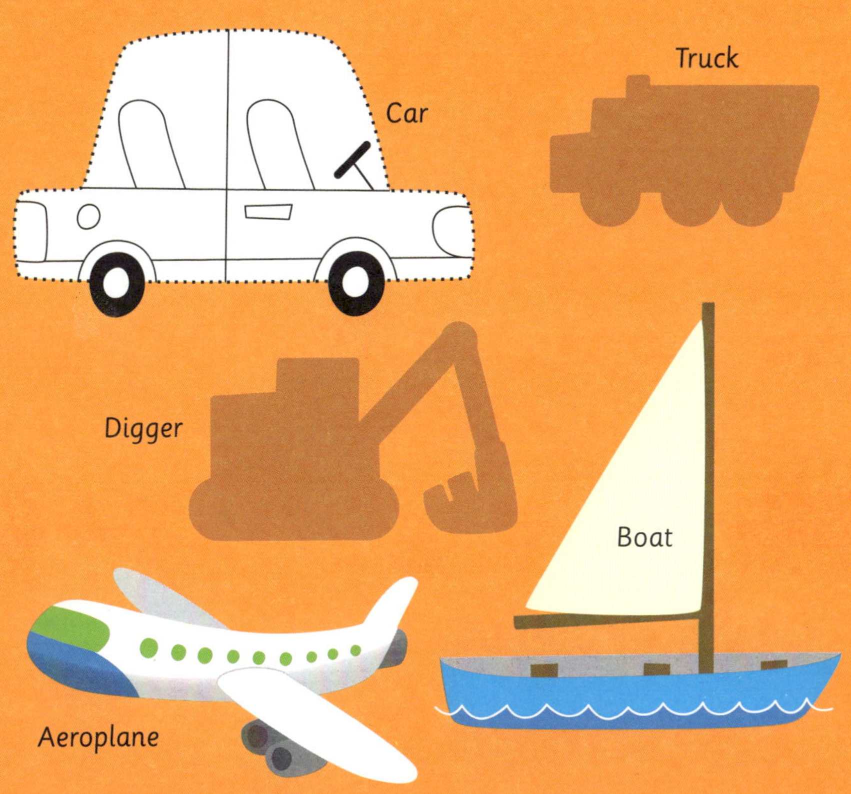

Family

Find the stickers, trace and colour in.

Pets

Find the stickers, trace and colour in.

Birthday

Find the stickers, trace and colour in.

Christmas

Find the stickers, trace and colour in.

Look back through the pages to see where these words appear.

In the
Wild

on the savannah
Can you find and circle five differences
between the two pictures?

Finger puppets

Ask a grown-up to cut them out.

Stick us to card
to make us strong!

finish the other activities first!

Sidney the snake

Trace over the dotted line to draw Sidney the snake, then colour him in.

Find the cloud stickers

Missing Spots

Can you help Giraffe as she has lost some spots?

Hungry hippo

Find some more teeth stickers so Harriet can have her supper.

Safari friends

Find the other animal stickers so
Ellie can play with her friends.

Little lion lost

Leo is lost! Can you help him back to mummy for a cuddle?

Arctic freeze

Can you circle the polar bears with your crayon?

All things green

Use your pencils and crayons to colour everything in.

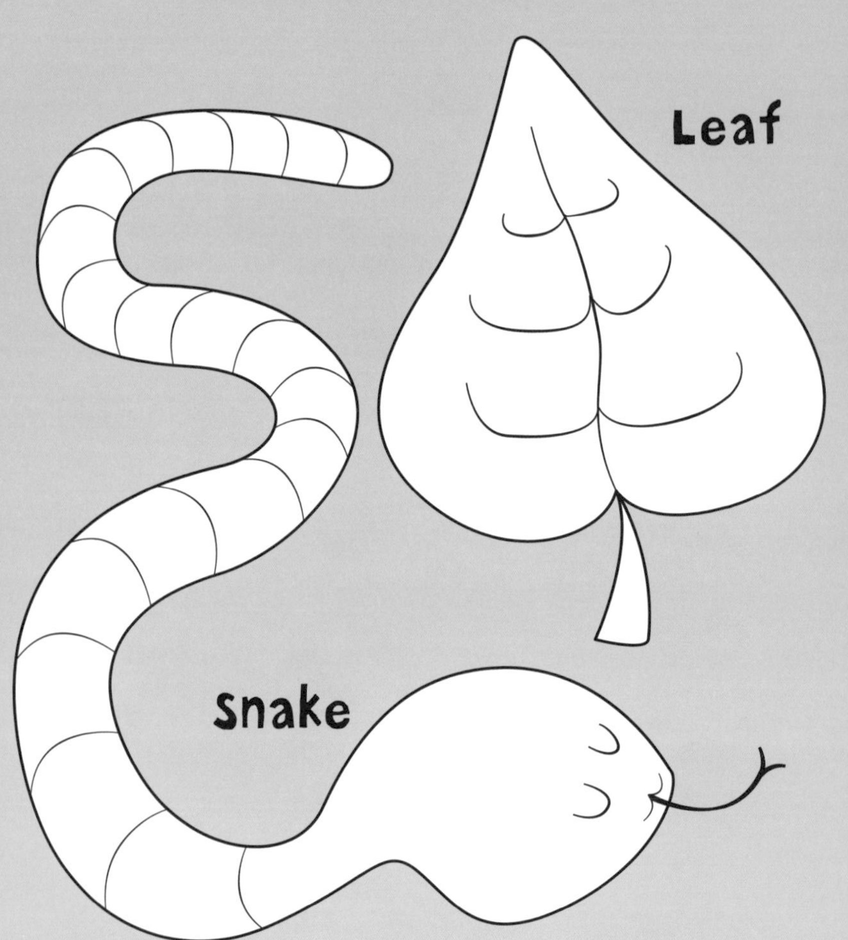

Parrot
Frog

Jungle pairs

Find the stickers then draw lines to join the matching pairs together.

superstar!
well done!

Winner!
Good job!

Winner!
Superstar!
1
2
3
4
5
6
7
8
9

Good job!
10
10

Baker

Good job!
Superstar!
Winner!

well done!

superstar!

Good job!
well done!

Winner!
Good job!

superstar!

superstar!
well done!

Winner!
Good job!

Good job!

well done!

well done!

superstar!
Winner!

superstar!
Good job!

colours

Red

Find the stickers, trace the lines and colour in all things red.

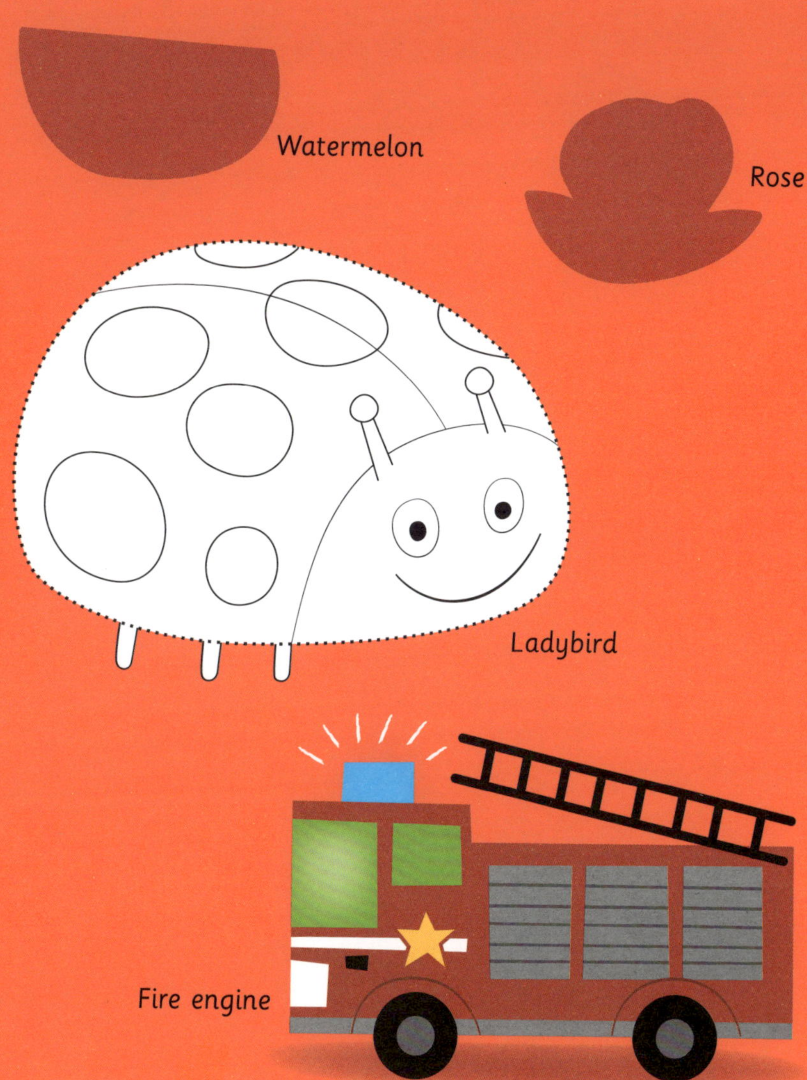
Watermelon
Rose
Ladybird
Fire engine

Blue

Find the stickers, trace the lines and colour in all things blue.

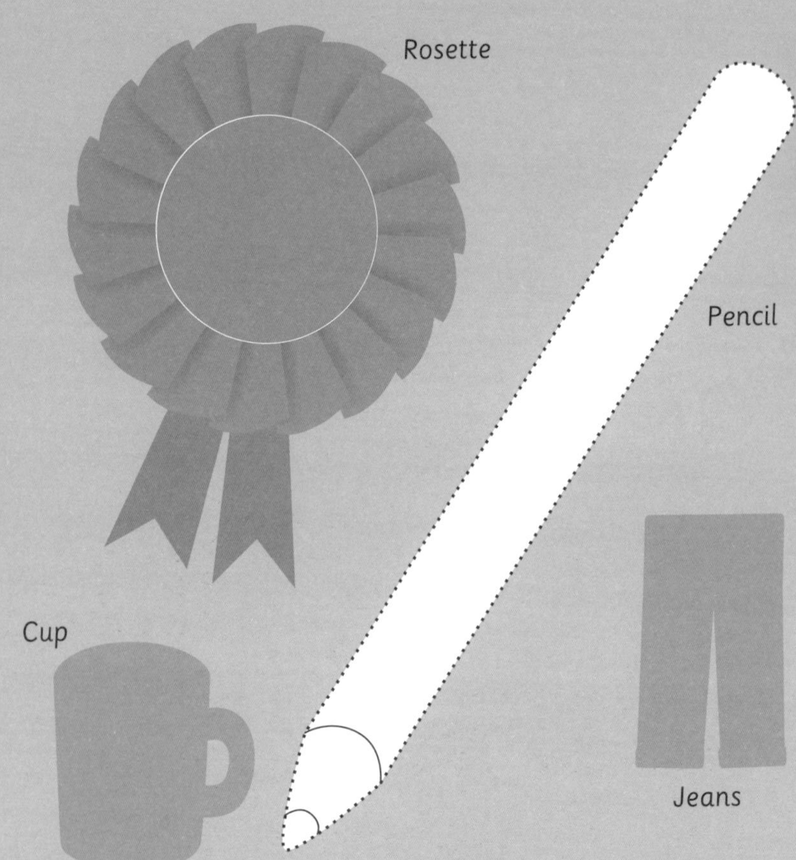

Balloon
Butterfly
Blue whale

Green

Find the stickers, trace the lines and colour in all things green.

Broccoli
Apple
Clover
Lime
Lizard

Yellow

Find the stickers, trace the lines and colour in all things yellow.

Sun
Banana
Sandcastle
Duckling
Sunflower

Purple

Find the stickers, trace the lines
and colour in all things purple.

Present

Flower

Monster

Grapes

Orange

Find the stickers, trace the lines and colour in all things orange.

Basketball
Lolly
Clownfish
Orangutan

Pink

Find the stickers, trace the lines and colour in all things pink.

Wellies
Flamingo
Princess
Tiara

Black

Find the stickers, trace the lines and colour in all things black.

Jack and the Beanstalk

Jack and the Beanstalk

Once upon a time there was a little boy called Jack who lived in a small village. They were very poor, so one day Jack's mother sent him to market to sell their cow

so they could buy some food. As he walked he met a man who asked Jack to swap the cow for some magic beans.

Jack agreed, and made his mother very angry when she found out that he had swapped Daisy the cow for some useless beans! She took them from Jack and threw them out the window.

The next morning, Jack looked out of his window to see a huge green beanstalk had grown in the garden! He got dressed and climbed up the beanstalk. When he got to the top he saw a magical castle that had a giant living there. Outside the castle, Jack met a fairy who told him that the giant had caught a goose that could lay golden eggs.

"If you rescue the goose all your problems will be solved," the fairy told Jack. So he climbed over the castle wall and hid in a cupboard while the giant ate his supper.

On the kitchen table,
Jack saw a big golden
goose sat in a cage.
He waited for the giant
to fall asleep and then
grabbed the cage, but
all the noise woke
the giant up!

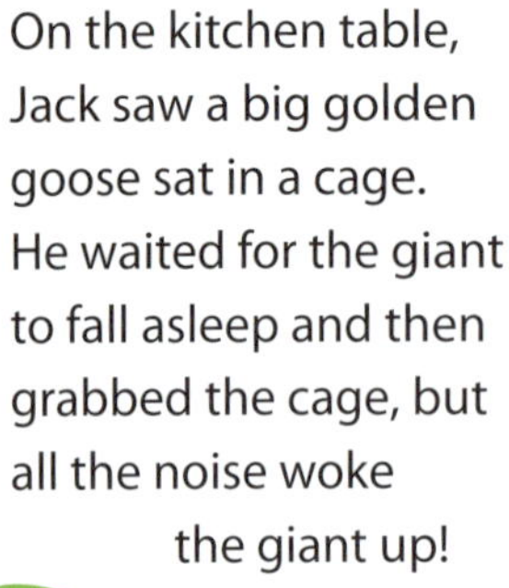

"Fee-fi-fo-fum! I smell the
blood of an Englishman!" He saw Jack and chased
after him out of the castle and down the
great beanstalk, shouting, "Fee-fi-fo-fum!
I smell the blood of an Englishman!" all the while.

After Jack got to the bottom of the beanstalk he ran to his house to get an axe. He chopped the beanstalk down before the giant could reach the bottom.

Now that Jack and his mother had the golden goose they never had to go hungry again, and lived happily ever after.

Daisy the cow

Trace over the dotted line to draw Daisy the cow, then colour her in.

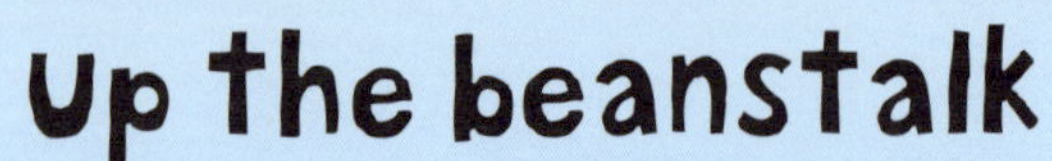

Up the beanstalk

Can you add some leaf stickers to the beanstalk to help Jack climb?

Scary GIANT!

Add some teeth stickers to the big bad giant.

The giant's castle
Can you find and circle five differences between the two pictures?

Help Jack escape

Help Jack find the goose so he can escape!

Dress-up Jack

Find the stickers to get Jack dressed.

The giant's kitchen

Use your crayons to colour in the scene.

Match for Jack

Find the stickers, then draw lines to join the matching pairs together.

Animals

Jungle

Find the stickers, join the dots and colour in to complete this group of jungle animals.

Frog
Butterfly
Toucan
Parrot
Lemur

Farm

Find the stickers, join the dots and colour in to complete this group of farm animals.

Sheep
Goat
Chicken
Cow
Ducklings

Ocean

Find the stickers, join the dots and colour in to complete this group of ocean animals.

Jellyfish
Crab
Turtle
Lobster
Shark

Pets

Find the stickers, join the dots and colour in to complete this group of pets.

Rabbit
Puppy
Guinea pig
Goldfish
Budgie

Zoo

Find the stickers, join the dots and colour in to complete this group of zoo animals.

Polar bear
Seal
Lion
Flamingo
Iguana

Animal Patterns

Find the stickers that match the patterns.

Giraffe
?
?
Zebra

Animal
Tracks

Find the stickers of the animal tracks.

Monkey
Cat
Ostrich

King of the Jungle

Colour in this lion to make him roar!

1
2
3
3
2
1
1
2
3
Numbers
1
2
3
3
2
1
1
2
3
3
2
1
1
2
3
3
2
1

One 1

Find the stickers, trace and colour in.

Two 2

Find the stickers, trace and colour in.

Three

3

Find the stickers, trace and colour in.

Four 4

Find the stickers, trace and colour in.

Five 5

Find the stickers, trace and colour in.

Six 6

Find the stickers, trace and colour in.

Seven

7

Find the stickers, trace and colour in.

7 Vegetables

7 Strawberries
7 Leaves

Eight 8

Find the stickers, trace and colour in.

8 Puppies

Nine 9

Find the stickers, trace and colour in.

9 Cupcakes

Ten 10

Find the stickers, trace and colour in.

10 Dolls

Can you write the correct number by each line?

Sea
Animals

Rock pool

Can you find and circle five differences between the two pictures?

Sunken treasure

This diver is looking for pearls,
can you help him find the treasure?

Shark attack!

Find some teeth stickers for the scary shark!

on the ocean bed

Colour in this scene and add stickers of the creatures that live there.

Penguin pairs

Add the stickers and trace the lines to the matching penguins.

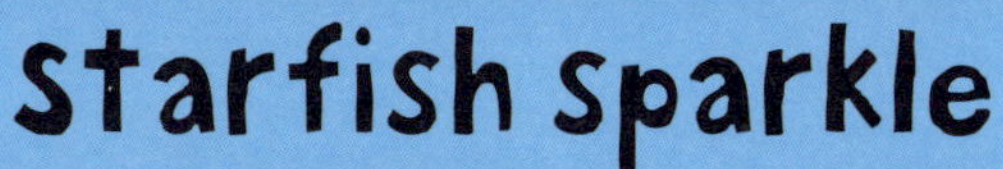

Starfish Sparkle

Join the dots, colour in and add some other starfish stickers

Pacific playtime!

Find the stickers so that clownfish has some friends to play with.

Sidney the seahorse

What colour should Sidney be?

Now colour him in.

Dancing dolphins!

Which dolphin is asleep at dance class?

All things blue

Use your pencils or crayons to colour everything in.

Rain

Ship
Whale

Matching friends

Can you draw lines between the matching friends?

The Three Little Pigs

The Three Little Pigs

Once upon a time there were three little pigs who left home to build three little houses in the woods.

The first pig was in a rush and built a house out of straw. The second pig built a house out of wood, and the third pig – who wanted to be very safe – built a house out of bricks.

One day the big bad wolf arrived in the woods. He stopped by the straw house first. "Let me in, let me in!" he shouted. "I won't! Not by the hairs on my chinny chin chin!" the little pig called back.

The wolf got very angry, "Then I'll huff and I'll puff, and I'll blow your house in!" So he huffed, and he puffed, and he blew the straw house down.

The little pig was scared and ran off to the wood house. Soon the wolf knocked on the door. "Let me in, let me in!" he howled. "We won't! Not by the hairs on our chinny chin chins!" the little pigs shouted.

The wolf was even more angry, "I'll huff and I'll puff, and I'll blow your house in!" So he huffed, and he puffed, and he blew the wooden house down.

The two little pigs ran to the brick house, but the wolf chased them and shouted, "Let me in, let me in!"

"We won't! Not by the hairs on our chinny chin chins!" the little pigs called back.

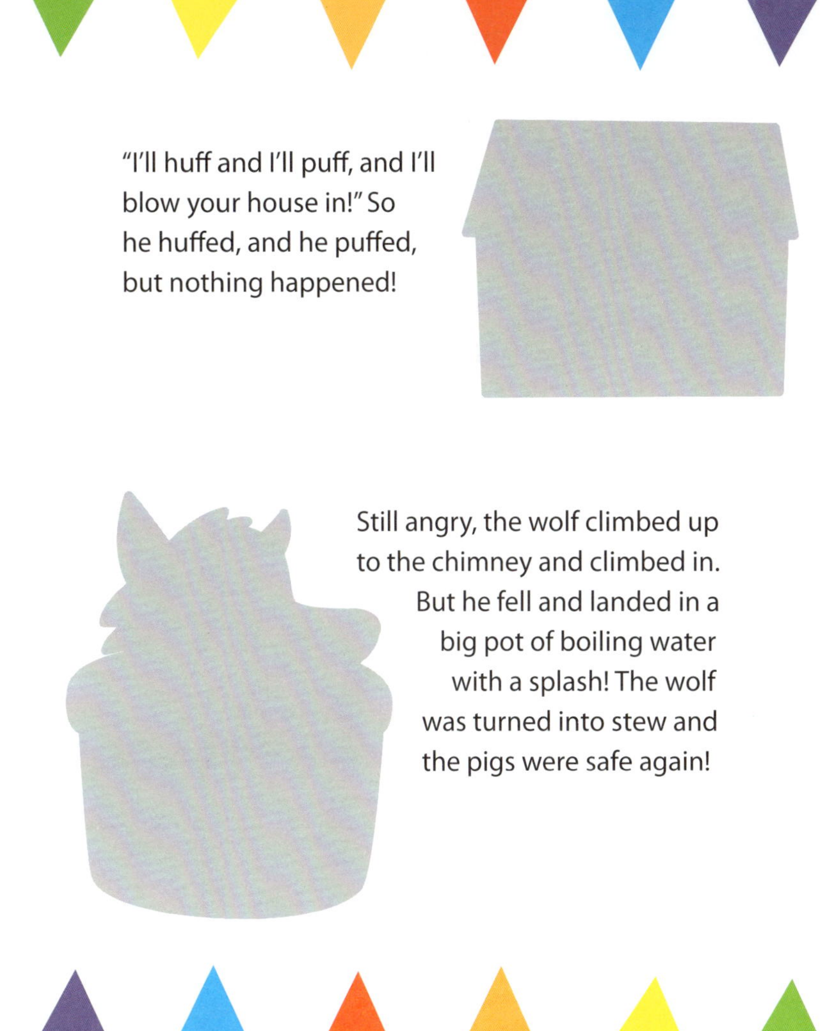

"I'll huff and I'll puff, and I'll blow your house in!" So he huffed, and he puffed, but nothing happened!

Still angry, the wolf climbed up to the chimney and climbed in. But he fell and landed in a big pot of boiling water with a splash! The wolf was turned into stew and the pigs were safe again!

Piggy's kitchen
Can you find and circle five differences
between the two pictures?

Missing tails

The three pigs' and wolf's tails are missing.
Find the stickers.

Blow your house down!

Join the dots so wolf can huff and puff!

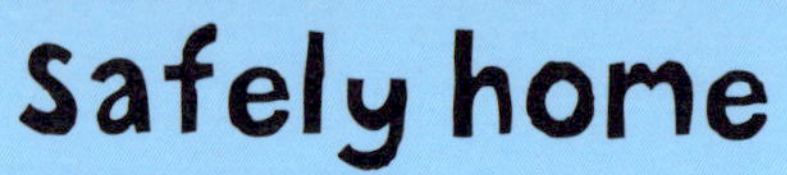

Safely home

Find the stickers of the pig's houses and add to the picture.

The hot pot

Find vegetable stickers to make the stew tasty!

Little pig is lost

Help little pig get home.
Which trail will lead him to his house?

Finger puppets

Ask a grown-up to cut us out.

Stick us to card
to make us strong!

finish the other activities first!

Playful pigs

Circle the pig that has a green bow-tie.